I0821671

PERSIAN CATS

abdopublishing.com

Published by Abdo Publishing, a division of ABDO, PO Box 398166, Minneapolis, Minnesota 55439.

Big Buddy Books™ is a trademark and logo of Abdo Publishing.

Printed in China.
092017
012018

Cover Photo: Getty Images.
Interior Photos: Getty Images (pp. 5, 7, 9, 11, 13, 15, 17, 19, 21, 23, 25, 27, 29, 30).

Coordinating Series Editor: Tamara L. Britton
Contributing Editor: Jill Roesler
Graphic Design: Jenny Christensen

Publisher's Cataloging-in-Publication Data

Names: Lajiness, Katie, author.
Title: Persian cats / by Katie Lajiness.
Description: Minneapolis, Minnesota : Abdo Publishing, 2018. | Series: Big buddy cats | Includes online resources and index.
Identifiers: LCCN 2017943923 | ISBN 9781532112010 (lib.bdg.) | ISBN 9781614799085 (ebook)
Subjects: LCSH: Persian cat--Juvenile literature. | Cats--Juvenile literature
Classification: DDC 636.832--dc23
LC record available at https://lccn.loc.gov/2017943923

CONTENTS

A POPULAR BREED

Cats are popular pets. About 35 percent of US households have a cat. And, Americans own more than 85 million!

Around the world, there are more than 40 **domestic cat breeds**. One of these is the Persian cat. Let's learn why the Persian is the fourth-most popular cat breed in the United States.

Actress Marilyn Monroe owned a white Persian cat like this one. Its name was Mitsou.

THE CAT FAMILY

All cats belong to the **Felidae** family. There are 37 **species** in this family. **Domestic cats** are part of one species. Lions and other types of cats make up the others.

Did you know?

Humans and cats have lived together for at least 3,500 years.

Modern cats do many of the same things as their ancient wildcat relatives. Both wiggle their rear ends to balance their paws before jumping.

PERSIAN CATS

As their name suggests, Persian cats came from a Middle Eastern country once called Persia. Around 1684 BC, the **breed** first appeared in **hieroglyphics**.

Persian cats arrived in Italy in 1620. At the same time, the breed made its way to France. Over hundreds of years, Persians spread throughout Europe.

Queen Victoria of England loved Persian cats. Blue Persians (*shown*) were her favorite.

The Persian **breed** came to the United States in the late 1800s. It quickly became the most popular kind of cat. And, it was one of the original breeds recognized by the **Cat Fanciers' Association**.

In 1871, Persians appeared in the world's first cat show.

WHAT THEY'RE LIKE

Persian cats are one of the least active **breeds**. Generally, they prefer to lie around and take naps. They like to sleep in the sun or lie on someone's lap. But they have moments when they act like kittens.

Persian cats have sweet, quiet natures. They easily fit in with families that have children and other pets.

COAT AND COLOR

Persian cats have beautiful coats. Sometimes, their coats will make them appear fat. But it's just their thick undercoat and long top coat that makes them look fluffy.

Did you know?

Persians have tufts of fur on their ears and paws.

Cats in this breed come in about 100 different color and pattern combinations.

SIZE

Persian cats have a different look. They have wide chests and short, strong bodies. These cats have large paws and fluffy tails.

Large heads and short **muzzles** are a **breed** standard. Their ears are small and rounded. Most adult males weigh more than 12 pounds (5 kg). Females are somewhat smaller.

Persian cats with white coats and blue eyes often cannot hear.

FEEDING

Healthy cat food includes beef, chicken, or fish. A good name-brand food will provide the **nutrients** a cat needs.

Cat food can be dry, semimoist, or canned. Food labels will show how much and how often to feed a cat.

Feed a cat from clean bowls. And set out a bowl of fresh water in an area away from the food dish.

CARE

Cats need regular care to keep them healthy. Persian cats have a lot of fur that can easily tangle. So, it is important to **groom** a Persian every day.

A Persian's tears can stain the fur on its flat face. So, this breed needs its face cleaned regularly.

Persian cats need a good veterinarian. The vet can provide health exams and **vaccines**. He or she can also **spay** or **neuter** cats.

Kittens need to see the vet several times during their first few months. Adult cats should visit the vet once a year for a checkup.

Did you know?

Use a cat carrier when taking a cat to the vet. This way, the cat feels safe and secure.

Persians have large, wide-set eyes. Their eyes may even be two different colors.

Cats have an **instinct** to bury their waste. So, cats should use a **litter box**. Waste should be removed from the box daily.

A cat buries its waste to mark its area. If a cat goes outdoors, it will begin to do the same. A **microchip** can help bring a cat home if it gets lost.

Cats like warm places to sleep. Place a blanket in a basket to create a cozy cat bed.

KITTENS

A Persian cat mother is **pregnant** for 63 to 65 days. Then, she gives birth to a **litter** of about four kittens. For the first two weeks, kittens mostly eat and sleep.

All kittens are born blind and deaf. After two weeks, they can see and hear. But, they still stay close to their mother to feel warm and safe. At three weeks, the kittens begin taking their first steps.

Kitten food is different than adult cat food. Food for kittens includes extra elements to help them grow to be healthy and strong.

THINGS THEY NEED

Between 12 and 16 weeks old, Persian kittens are ready for **adoption**. Kittens like to be active. So, they need daily exercise. A Persian cat will be a loving companion for about 15 years.

Keep a kitten's bed in a quiet place. This way, it will get plenty of rest.

GLOSSARY

adoption the process of taking responsibility for a pet.

breed a group of animals sharing the same appearance and features. To breed is to produce animals by mating.

Cat Fanciers' Association established in 1906, it is the world's largest registry for pedigreed cats.

domestic cats tame cats that make great pets.

Felidae the scientific Latin name for the cat family. Members of this family are called felines. They include domestic cats, lions, tigers, lynx, and cheetahs.

groom to clean and care for.

hieroglyphic any of the symbols in the picture writing of ancient Egypt.

instinct a way of behaving, thinking, or feeling that is not learned, but natural.

litter all of the kittens born at one time to a mother cat.

litter box a place for house cats to leave their waste.

microchip an electronic circuit placed under an animal's skin. A microchip contains identifying information that can be read by a scanner.

muzzle an animal's nose and jaws.

neuter (NOO-tuhr) to remove a male animal's reproductive glands.

nutrient (NOO-tree-uhnt) something found in food that living beings take in to live and grow.

pregnant having one or more babies growing within the body.

spay to remove a female animal's reproductive organs.

species (SPEE-sheez) living things that are very much alike.

vaccine (vak-SEEN) a shot given to prevent illness or disease.

ONLINE RESOURCES

To learn more about Persian cats, visit **abdobooklinks.com**. These links are routinely monitored and updated to provide the most current information available.

INDEX